D1249756

WORLD COMMODITIES

Oil

GARRY CHAPMAN » GARY HODGES

Smart Apple Media
P.O. Box 3263
Mankato, MN, 56002

First published in 2010 by
MACMILLAN EDUCATION AUSTRALIA PTY LTD
15–19 Claremont Street, South Yarra 3141

Visit our web site at www.macmillan.com.au or go directly to www.macmillanlibrary.com.au

Associated companies and representatives throughout the world.

Copyright © Garry Chapman and Gary Hodges 2010

Library of Congress Cataloging-in-Publication Data

Chapman, Garry.
  Oil / Garry Chapman and Gary Hodges.
     p. cm. — (World commodities)
  Includes index.
  ISBN 978-1-59920-586-1 (library binding)
  1. Petroleum industry and trade—Juvenile literature. 2. Petroleum—Juvenile literature. I. Hodges, Gary. II. Title.
  HD9565.C53 2011
  338.2'7282—dc22

                              2010007308

Publisher: Carmel Heron   Designer: Ivan Finnegan (cover and text)
Commissioning Editor: Niki Horin   Page Layout: Ivan Finnegan
Managing Editor: Vanessa Lanaway   Photo Researcher: Lesya Bryndzia (management: Debbie Gallagher)
Editor: Laura Jeanne Gobal   Illustrators: Andy Craig and Nives Porcellato, **14**, **15**, **19**; Alan Laver, **13**, **17**, **28**
Proofreader: Kirstie Innes-Will   Production Controller: Vanessa Johnson

Manufactured in the United States of America by Corporate Graphics, Minnesota.
052010

Acknowledgments
The author and the publisher are grateful to the following for permission to reproduce copyright material:

Front cover photograph of an off-shore oil rig: Shutterstock/maksimum

Alamy/Lourens Smak, **5**; Corbis/Gary Braasch, **22**, /CNP/Ron Sachs, **12** (bottom), /EPA/Barbara Gindl, **9** (top left), /Lowell Georgia, **11** (top), /Gerd Ludwig, **11** (2nd bottom), /Science Faction/NASA, **27**, /Scott T. Smith, **12** (top), /Ted Soqui, **26**, /George Steinmetz, **10** (middle), /Keith Wood, **10** (top), /Xinhua Press/Li Zhen, **21**; Getty Images/AFP/Michel Gangne, **9** (top right), /James P. Blair, **23**, /Peter Dazeley, **29**, /Hulton Archive, **8**, /Dorling Kindersley, **4** (iron ore), /Scott Peterson, **25**, /Yngve Rakke, **18**, /Jacob Silberberg, **24**; iStockphoto/Igor Grochev, **7**, /Peter Ingvorsen, **10** (bottom); Photolibrary/David Halpern, **11** (bottom); Reuters/Ho New, **20**; Shutterstock/Forest Badger, **4** (oil), /Epic Stock, **11** (2nd top), /IDAL, **4** (wheat), /LLEPOD, **9** (bottom), /Worldpics, **4** (coal), /yykkaa, **4** (sugar), /Magdalena Zurawska, **4** (coffee).

While every care has been taken to trace and acknowledge copyright, the publisher tenders their apologies for any accidental infringement where copyright has proved untraceable. Where the attempt has been unsuccessful, the publisher welcomes information that would redress the situation.

Please note: At the time of printing, the Internet addresses appearing in this book were correct. Owing to the dynamic nature of the Internet, however, we cannot guarantee that all of these addresses will remain correct.

This series is for my father, Ron Chapman, with gratitude. – Garry Chapman

This series is dedicated to the memory of Jean and Alex Ross, as well as my immediate family of Sue, Hannah and Jessica, my parents, Jim and Val, and my brother Leigh. – Gary Hodges

Contents

Glossary Words

When a word is printed in **bold**, you can look up its meaning in the Glossary on page 31.

What Is a World Commodity?

A commodity is any product for which someone is willing to pay money. A world commodity is a product that is traded across the world.

The World's Most Widely Traded Commodities

Many of the world's most widely traded commodities are **agricultural** products, such as coffee, sugar, and wheat, or **natural resources**, such as coal, iron ore, and oil. These commodities are produced in large amounts by people around the world.

Coal, coffee, iron ore, oil, sugar, and wheat are important commodities traded around the world.

Commodities and the World's Economy

Whenever the world's **demand** for a commodity increases or decreases, the price of this commodity goes up or down by the same amount everywhere. Prices usually vary from day to day. The daily trade in world commodities plays a key role in the state of the world's **economy**.

MORE ABOUT...
The Quality of Commodities

When people, businesses, or countries buy a commodity, they assume that its quality will be consistent. Oil is an example of a commodity. When people trade in oil, all barrels of oil are considered to be of the same quality regardless of where they come from.

Oil Is a Commodity

Oil is a natural resource and a major source of energy. It is needed for transportation and to power industries, heat buildings, and manufacture chemicals and plastics. It is used in every country on Earth.

A Fossil Fuel

Oil comes from a fossil fuel known as petroleum. Fossil fuels were formed over millions of years, when the remains of plants and animals became trapped under layers of **sediment**. Eventually, high levels of heat and pressure forced physical and chemical changes in the plant and animal remains, transforming them into fossil fuels.

Most oil is used in the production of fuel to power vehicles.

What Is In Petroleum?

Petroleum comprises liquid crude oil and also natural gas. Crude oil is a dark, flammable liquid usually found deep beneath Earth's surface. It can also be found in tar sands (heavy deposits of crude oil, water and clay or sand) and oil shale (a type of rock).

COMMODITY FACT!

Extracting oil from tar sands requires up to four barrels of water for each barrel of oil produced.

Where Is Oil Found and Where Is It Used?

Oil is found in vast underground reservoirs, trapped between layers of rock. It is not found all over the world, only in certain places where the conditions were favorable for this fossil fuel to form.

The Middle East

About two-thirds of the world's known oil reserves are in the Middle East. The largest oil producer in the world is Saudi Arabia. Other producers in the region include Iraq, Kuwait, Qatar, and the United Arab Emirates (UAE). Underground oil reservoirs in this region are vast and easy to extract.

Other Oil-producing Regions

The world's second-largest oil-producing region is North America, where oil is found in Canada, the United States, and Mexico. Countries such as Russia, China, Norway, and Venezuela are also major producers of oil.

THE WORLD'S MAJOR PRODUCERS OF OIL (2008)

Country	Amount of Oil Produced (barrels per day)	Percentage of Total World Production
Saudi Arabia	11 million	13.9%
Russia	9.9 million	12.5%
United States	8.3 million	10.5%
Iran	4.2 million	5.3%
Mexico	3.8 million	4.8%

The Organization of the Petroleum Exporting Countries

The Organization of the Petroleum Exporting Countries (OPEC) consists of 13 oil-producing countries from the Middle East, Africa, and South America. OPEC coordinates its oil production activities to ensure that there is always a ready **supply** of oil available. This helps to keep prices stable and ensures that OPEC members are well paid for the oil they **export**.

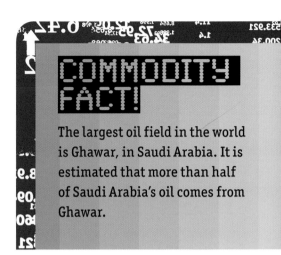

COMMODITY FACT!

The largest oil field in the world is Ghawar, in Saudi Arabia. It is estimated that more than half of Saudi Arabia's oil comes from Ghawar.

Oil Consumers

The world's main oil consumers are **developed countries**, such as the United States, Japan, France, and Germany. **Developing countries**, such as China and India, also need large amounts of oil to fuel their growing industries.

Large oil tankers are used to transport oil from where it is found to where it is used.

The United States

Although the United States is a major producer of oil, it still **imports** oil from other countries for its own consumption. This is because it uses more oil than it produces. The United States, with its many industries and transportation requirements, is the world's largest consumer of oil.

Timeline: **The History of Oil**

Oil products have been used by humans for more than 4,000 years in construction and for lighting and heating.

about 2000 B.C.
Ancient craftsmen use asphalt, a sticky black substance found in oil, in the construction of ships and buildings. Oil products are also used to attach arrowheads and preserve bodies.

1858
North America's first oil well is dug at Oil Springs in Ontario, Canada, by James Miller Williams.

1859
The oil industry in the United States begins when Edwin Drake drills a well at Oil Creek, near Titusville, Pennsylvania.

1861
Russia's first refinery is built in the Baku oil fields. Baku produces about 90 percent of the world's oil.

2000 B.C.

1846
Abraham Pineo Gesner develops a process of refining liquid kerosene from coal. This produces a cheap, clean heating fuel. It gains popularity across North America. Gesner becomes known as the founder of the modern oil industry.

In the late 1800s and early 1900s, oil **derricks** were a familiar sight along some highways in the United States.

A.D. **1745**
Oil sands are mined at Merkwiller-Pechelbronn in Alsace, France. This region produces oil until 1970.

1854
Benjamin Silliman becomes the first person to distill oil into different products. Silliman's discovery paves the way for the construction of oil refineries.

The first well to extract oil from rock is built in Bóbrka, Poland.

about 1880
The need for heating and lighting fuel leads to the establishment of oil wells in California, Oklahoma, and Texas, as well as other places in Eastern Europe.

During the Gulf War (1990–1991), Iraqi forces burned oil fields in Kuwait.

about 1900
The introduction of the internal combustion engine creates a huge demand for oil. The engine is used to power industries and transportation.

1956
Scientist M. King Hubbert predicts that oil production in the United States will peak around 1971.

2000s
Middle Eastern countries are the world's leading producers of oil, but political conflicts and wars lead to oil shortages and price increases. People start to drive fuel-efficient cars.

1920s
Affordable cars and improved roads lead to widespread car ownership. A ready supply of gasoline is needed and the oil trade booms.

1979
An energy crisis is created by the Iranian Revolution. Less oil is exported by this country, sending prices up. This sparks the development of fuel-efficient cars and home insulation in an attempt to reduce the reliance on oil.

A.D. 2006

about 1955
Oil replaces coal as the world's most important source of energy.

1970
M. King Hubbert's prediction comes true. The United States reaches peak oil. OPEC takes the opportunity to manipulate oil prices, leading to crises in 1973 and 1979. Since then, other countries have also peaked.

2006
There is a strong possibility that Russia, formerly a major oil producer, has reached its maximum rate of oil extraction.

1910s
Oil production spreads around the world. Significant oil fields operate in Canada, Indonesia, Iran, Mexico, Peru, and Venezuela.

1960
OPEC is formed to represent some oil-producing countries in Africa, the Middle East, and South America.

In the 1800s, kerosene was burned in lamps to produce light.

OPEC's headquarters is in Vienna, Austria.

How Is Oil Drilled?

The world's demand for oil is so great that oil companies must continue searching for new oil reservoirs. They use satellite images to determine possible areas to explore and then employ **geologists** to study the **terrain**.

Exploration

A location is identified as possibly containing oil. Geologists conduct tests to find oil reservoirs.

Drilling

Holes are drilled into the ground or seabed to discover the extent of the reservoir. The greater the company's success rate at finding oil, the cheaper the oil products will eventually be for the consumer.

Production Facilities and Pipelines

Legal teams get permission for the oil company to drill the ground or seabed, and production facilities and pipelines are constructed to extract the oil and carry it away.

Preparing for Transportation
Once the oil starts flowing to the surface, the drilling equipment is replaced by a pump, which controls the rate of flow. Oil is pumped into an oil tanker or pipeline and transported to a refinery.

Bringing the Oil to the Surface
A tube is inserted to form a well and the surrounding area between the tube and the casing is sealed, forcing the oil to flow only through the well. Often, underground pressure forces oil up the well to the surface, but it may be necessary to use a pump to help the oil flow.

Reaching the Oil
Drilling continues deeper into the ground, with new sections of casing and pipe inserted at regular intervals. When oil begins to appear in the mud that reaches the surface, tests are conducted to determine if the oil reservoir has been reached.

Heavy Drilling
A derrick is erected over a large hole, in which a large pipe is inserted, supported by a casing. The drill is lowered into this pipe in sections that join together. The drill bit, which is at the bottom, has sharp "teeth" made of diamonds. As the drill turns, it cuts into the earth. The waste it creates, a mix of rock and liquid, is pushed up the pipe and removed.

Refining Oil

When oil leaves the well, it is not in a form that can be used. It has to be sent to a refinery, where it is separated into different **fractions** and impurities are removed.

Getting Oil to the Refinery

Refineries are often located close to where oil is consumed, so that production can match demand. There are two main ways of getting oil to a refinery: pipelines and oil tankers.

Pipelines

If oil has to be transported over land to a refinery, it travels through a long pipeline, often crossing borders into neighboring countries.

The Trans-Alaska Pipeline carries oil across the state of Alaska.

This is the Saudi-owned Very Large Crude Carrier MV *Sirius Star*.

COMMODITY FACT!

Oil contains different **organic compounds** known as hydrocarbons, which are molecules of hydrogen and carbon in a range of combinations.

Oil Tankers

If oil has to cross oceans, it is transported in ships. Oil from the Middle East travels around the world in massive oil tankers called Very Large Crude Carriers. These ships are too large to enter many ports, so the oil is often transferred to smaller vessels while at sea, for the final part of the journey to the refinery.

Fractional Distillation

The different fractions that make up oil have different boiling points.
This means they can be separated by heating the oil to different
temperatures. This process is called fractional distillation.

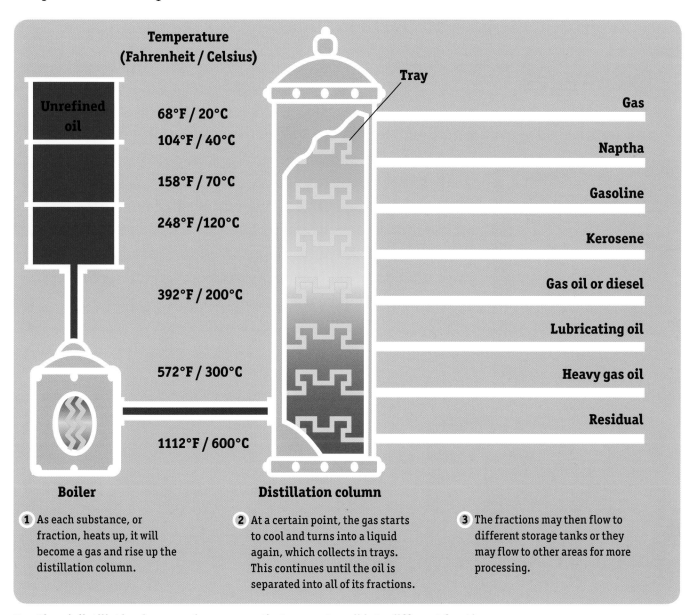

**Temperature
(Fahrenheit / Celsius)**

68°F / 20°C	Gas
104°F / 40°C	Naptha
158°F / 70°C	Gasoline
248°F /120°C	Kerosene
392°F / 200°C	Gas oil or diesel
	Lubricating oil
572°F / 300°C	Heavy gas oil
	Residual
1112°F / 600°C	

Tray

Unrefined oil

Boiler

Distillation column

1 As each substance, or fraction, heats up, it will become a gas and rise up the distillation column.

2 At a certain point, the gas starts to cool and turns into a liquid again, which collects in trays. This continues until the oil is separated into all of its fractions.

3 The fractions may then flow to different storage tanks or they may flow to other areas for more processing.

Fractional distillation is a complex process that separates oil into different fractions.

The Oil Trade

Oil is the most actively traded commodity in the world. Many industries and transportation would not function without oil. A high percentage of all vehicles on the road runs on fuels made from oil.

Exchanges

An exchange is a place where commodities, such as oil, are bought and sold. At an exchange, oil is bought and sold in both the spot market and futures market.

COMMODITY FACT!

The New York Mercantile Exchange is a busy place. In April 2008, 1.7 million oil contracts on average were traded there every day.

The Spot Market

In the spot market, buyers and sellers agree on a price for the immediate exchange of goods. This means oil is delivered to the buyer as soon as it is purchased. Once the price is paid, the oil is transported from the refinery to the place where it will be used, such as a power plant.

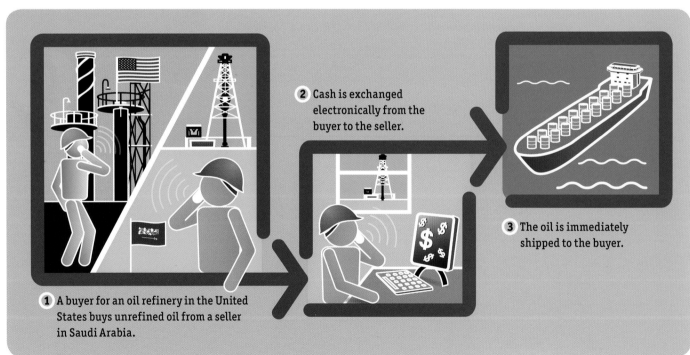

2 Cash is exchanged electronically from the buyer to the seller.

3 The oil is immediately shipped to the buyer.

1 A buyer for an oil refinery in the United States buys unrefined oil from a seller in Saudi Arabia.

The spot trading of oil is a simple transaction between an oil drilling company and an oil refinery, which takes place in three main stages.

The Futures Market

Trading in the futures market involves buying and selling contracts that are set in the future. Buyers and sellers agree on a price, which will be paid when the oil is delivered at a date in the future.

Futures oil trades are usually based on the purchase and delivery of a shipment of oil one month after the contract is sold. A futures oil trader buys the oil with the intention of selling it to someone else in the future for a better price. The trader tries to predict how the market price will change, hoping to make a profit on the deal.

> *"Everyone in the market for physical oil … is looking for that precious piece of information that will allow them to sell oil for more, or buy for less."*
>
> **Eivind Lie, oil trader, StatoilHydro**
> (Source: http://news.bbc.co.uk/2/hi/business/7250554.stm)

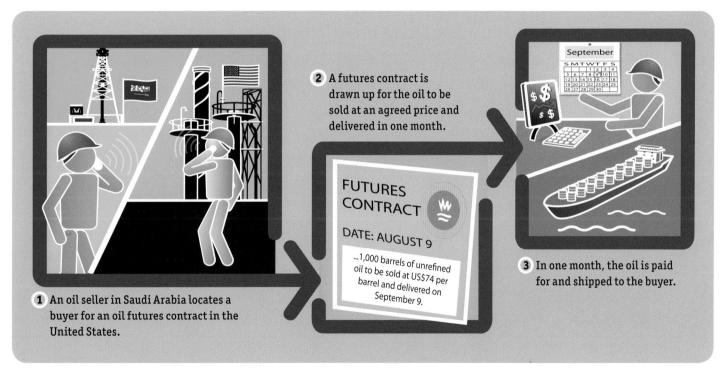

2. A futures contract is drawn up for the oil to be sold at an agreed price and delivered in one month.

FUTURES CONTRACT

DATE: AUGUST 9

…1,000 barrels of unrefined oil to be sold at US$74 per barrel and delivered on September 9.

1. An oil seller in Saudi Arabia locates a buyer for an oil futures contract in the United States.

3. In one month, the oil is paid for and shipped to the buyer.

The futures trading of oil takes place in three main stages. The oil refinery is agreeing to buy oil at a future date for a set price.

Supply and Demand

The oil trade is determined by supply and demand. When consumers are eager to buy the commodity, the demand for oil increases. Consumers rely on producers to supply it.

Factors Affecting Supply

There are many factors affecting the supply of oil.

- OPEC can control the global supply of oil by limiting the amount of oil produced by its member countries.
- Armed conflict can occur in major oil-producing regions, such as the Middle East.
- Natural disasters, such as earthquakes and hurricanes, can disrupt oil drilling and transportation.

Factors Affecting Demand

Similarly, there are many factors affecting the demand for oil.

- The aviation industry uses a lot of jet fuel. When people fly more, airlines use more jet fuel, and the demand for oil will go up.
- Oil and its products are important to many industries. The stronger a country's industrial sector, the higher its demand for oil will be, and the more oil it will import.
- High oil prices can force countries to use less oil and look for alternative sources of energy.

THE WORLD'S TOP EXPORTERS AND IMPORTERS OF OIL (2008)

Exporter	Number of Barrels Exported (Per Day)	Importer	Number of Barrels Imported (Per Day)
Saudi Arabia	8.4 million	United States	11 million
Russia	6.9 million	Japan	4.7 million
United Arab Emirates	2.5 million	China	3.9 million
Iran	2.4 million	Germany	2.4 million
Kuwait	2.4 million	South Korea	2.1 million

Price Variations

When the demand for oil is greater than the amount oil companies can supply, the price of oil increases. In the same way, when there is more oil supplied than the overall demand for it, the price of oil falls.

THE RISE AND FALL OF THE WORLD PRICE OF OIL

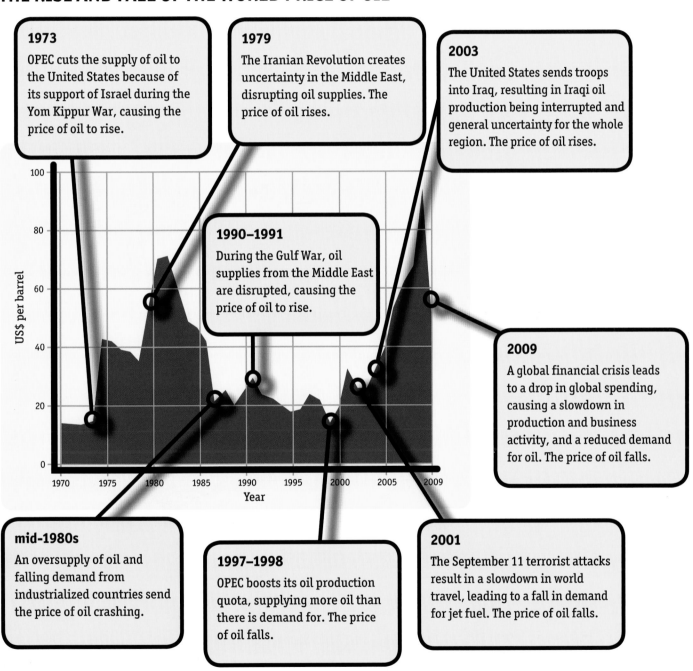

1973
OPEC cuts the supply of oil to the United States because of its support of Israel during the Yom Kippur War, causing the price of oil to rise.

1979
The Iranian Revolution creates uncertainty in the Middle East, disrupting oil supplies. The price of oil rises.

2003
The United States sends troops into Iraq, resulting in Iraqi oil production being interrupted and general uncertainty for the whole region. The price of oil rises.

1990–1991
During the Gulf War, oil supplies from the Middle East are disrupted, causing the price of oil to rise.

2009
A global financial crisis leads to a drop in global spending, causing a slowdown in production and business activity, and a reduced demand for oil. The price of oil falls.

mid-1980s
An oversupply of oil and falling demand from industrialized countries send the price of oil crashing.

1997–1998
OPEC boosts its oil production quota, supplying more oil than there is demand for. The price of oil falls.

2001
The September 11 terrorist attacks result in a slowdown in world travel, leading to a fall in demand for jet fuel. The price of oil falls.

The world price of oil experiences highs and lows over time. Events around the world influence the supply of and demand for the commodity, which changes the price.

Codes of Practice

Codes of practice govern the way most commodities are traded internationally. The purpose of these codes is to ensure that commodities, such as oil, are fairly priced and traded.

International Conventions

Although the oil trade is largely unregulated, there are international conventions that govern the exploration, production, and distribution of oil. They aim to ensure that activities carried out by the oil industry do not harm human communities or natural **ecosystems**.

A number of countries drill for oil in the North Sea. Countries that are part of Marpol must ensure their oil drilling and shipping activities do not pollute the marine environment.

The Marpol Convention

The Marpol Convention attempts to protect the marine environment from all forms of oil pollution generated by ships. Marine oil spills can have devastating effects on the environment. Marpol was enacted in 1973 and 1978, and signed by 136 countries.

Oil Speculation

Oil speculation involves commodity traders buying oil contracts in the short term, with a plan to sell them at a future date when the price of oil rises. By doing this, oil speculators can make large profits. However, oil speculation can have an effect on price, and this affects the price that all oil buyers, including refineries, have to pay. This can have a trickle-down effect on the price of important everyday products, such as gasoline. Because of the effects of oil speculation, there have been moves to introduce more regulation to the oil industry.

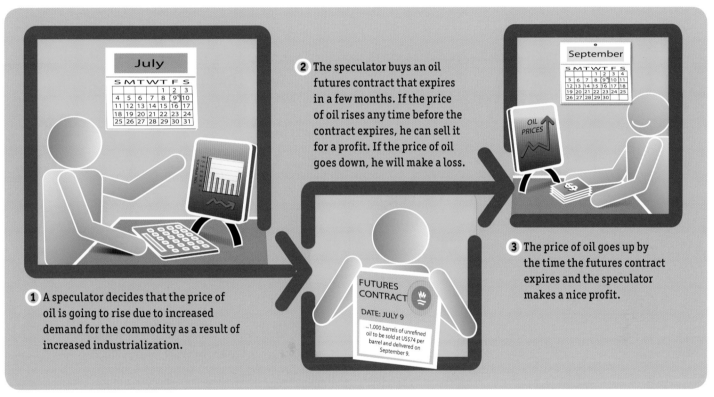

1 A speculator decides that the price of oil is going to rise due to increased demand for the commodity as a result of increased industrialization.

2 The speculator buys an oil futures contract that expires in a few months. If the price of oil rises any time before the contract expires, he can sell it for a profit. If the price of oil goes down, he will make a loss.

FUTURES CONTRACT
DATE: JULY 9
...1,000 barrels of unrefined oil to be sold at US$74 per barrel and delivered on September 9.

3 The price of oil goes up by the time the futures contract expires and the speculator makes a nice profit.

Speculators who trade in oil futures can make a lot of money. However, this trading is usually regulated so that the world price of oil is not pushed too high.

Commodity Futures Trading Commission

In 1975, the United States government set up the Commodity Futures Trading Commission (CFTC). The CFTC aimed to make the trading of commodities in the futures market open and honest, as well as competitive. In 2008, when oil prices climbed sharply, it was suspected that oil speculation was to blame. To counteract this, the CFTC implemented measures to reduce the amount of speculation in the **domestic** energy-futures market.

International Politics and Oil

The location of oil reserves and the countries that control them are important factors in the global oil trade. The decisions made by oil-rich countries often have widespread effects. The success of the leaders of oil-producing countries is often determined by the oil trade.

Venezuela: Hugo Chávez

Hugo Chávez was elected president of Venezuela in 1998. He wields significant power throughout Latin America. President Chávez's powerful position is strengthened by Venezuela's oil-generated wealth. The country is estimated to have the fifth-largest oil reserves in the world.

Oil accounts for half of the money earned by Venezuela and about one-third of the total market value of all goods and services produced in the country each year. The government-owned oil company Petróleos de Venezuela dominates the country's domestic oil market.

Venezeula has some of the largest oil reserves in the world, which means that President Chávez plays an important role in the oil trade.

COMMODITY FACT!

Venezuela has enough oil reserves to keep pumping oil for another 100 years!

Increasing the Price of Oil

Through Venezuela's membership of the Organization of the Petroleum Exporting Countries (OPEC), President Chávez has recommended that the price of oil be fixed at a higher level. This would benefit oil-producing countries but could damage the world's economy.

Saudi Arabia: King Abdullah bin Abdul Aziz al-Saud

King Abdullah bin Abdul Aziz al-Saud is the ruler of Saudi Arabia. He is one of the world's wealthiest men and occupies a position of global importance. His country currently controls about one-quarter of the world's known oil reserves. As a key member of OPEC and the biggest exporter of oil in the Middle East, Saudi Arabia has been influential in shaping world oil prices. The King's recommendations to either cut or boost Saudi oil production have a major impact on levels of global economic activity.

Oil-generated Wealth

Saudi Arabia has formed relationships with other emerging countries, such as China and India, to help them meet their increasing oil needs. Wealth generated from trading oil has funded a number of large-scale domestic projects throughout Saudi Arabia. King Abdullah also plays a key role in ongoing negotiations with other world leaders aimed at resolving regional conflicts in the Middle East.

Saudi Arabia's massive oil reserves have made King Abdullah one of the world's most powerful men.

Environmental Issues and Oil

The exploration, production, and distribution of oil sometimes have harmful effects on the environment. Oil spills and pipeline ruptures have caused major losses of wildlife and **habitat**, and gasoline-burning vehicles contribute to air pollution.

Oil Spills at Sea

Oil spills are a serious form of pollution. Oil spills at sea can be caused by tankers colliding or running aground, faulty equipment, and human carelessness. They can also happen during the extraction of oil from the sea. Oil spills can take years to clean up and their effects are widespread. Birds and marine animals that get covered by the oil can find it difficult to move or to stay warm. Oil also prevents sunlight from reaching plants beneath the water, affecting **photosynthesis**, which is important to all life on Earth.

This bird has been coated with oil from an oil spill. Rescue workers need to clean the oil from the bird's feathers if it is to survive.

MORE ABOUT...
The *Exxon Valdez* Oil Spill

In 1989, a ship called the *Exxon Valdez* struck a reef off the coast of Canada, releasing 10.5 million gallons (40 million l) of oil into the sea. The oil spill spread over 1,300 square miles (3,367 square km) of ocean. Reports indicate that as many as 500,000 seabirds may have died as a result of the spill.

Oil Spills on Land

On land, oil spills can be caused by breaks and ruptures in oil pipelines. One small hole, no larger than a small coin, can result in thousands of barrels of oil being lost and polluting the surrounding environment.

"We understand that to reduce our dependence on oil and the damage caused by climate change, we're going to need more production in the short term, we're going to need more efficiency, and we need more incentives for clean energy."

United States President Barack Obama
(Source: www.whitehouse.gov/the-press-office/remarks-president-business-roundtable)

In the Amazon rain forest of Brazil, large areas need to be cleared in order to drill for oil. This means that habitats are lost and there are fewer trees to absorb the greenhouse gas carbon dioxide.

Air Pollution

The burning of fossil fuels and their products releases **greenhouse gases**, which are harmful to the atmosphere. Gasoline, which is made from oil and used by vehicles, emits a gas called carbon monoxide when burned in engines. This gas not only contributes to air pollution, but is also dangerous to human and animal health. Other pollutants, such as sulfur dioxide, can also be released directly into the atmosphere during the oil-production process.

Social Issues and Oil

Oil has often been discovered in remote corners of the world. When oil-drilling operations come to remote regions, the lives of local communities are sometimes drastically changed.

Protecting Local Communities

The oil business is often very profitable. However, local communities do not always benefit from the wealth that comes with the discovery of oil in their area. In fact, sometimes the people who live closest to the oil fields may suffer as a result of oil production.

Nigeria's Ogoni People

Since the 1970s, the Ogoni people of Nigeria have suffered as a result of oil production in their traditional lands. Their lands have been affected by oil spills, their water contaminated by soot from **gas flares**, and their health affected by air pollution. Communities such as the Ogoni need to be protected by both their government and oil companies, to ensure that oil production in their area is fair for everyone involved.

This mangrove swamp in Goi, Nigeria, has been contaminated with oil from nearby drilling. This makes it difficult for the Ogoni people to find clean water for drinking and fishing.

Relocating Communities

Sometimes, governments that want to profit from oil reserves in their country may move entire communities away from their traditional lands to make way for oil-drilling operations. These relocated communities may end up with fewer job opportunities in their new homes, may not be able to farm the new land they find themselves occupying, and may be separated from their extended families.

Iraq's Kurdish People

Since the discovery of oil in the region, Kirkuk's oil fields have been an important natural resource for Iraq. The region produces almost 1 million barrels per day and is responsible for nearly half of the country's export earnings. Since the 1970s, Kurdish farming families have been forced to leave their traditional homelands near the Kirkuk oil fields, to live in areas hundreds of miles away.

This Kurdish girl, expelled from her home in Kirkuk, sits by a tent in the camp she and her family have been relocated to.

Is the Oil Industry Sustainable?

To sustain something is to keep it going for a very long time. There are three aspects to keeping the oil industry sustainable: maintaining the demand for oil; protecting the environment from the effects of oil exploration, extraction, and refining; and making sure oil producers can survive when oil runs out.

A Nonrenewable Resource

Oil is readily available around the world and will be so for some time. However, oil is a **nonrenewable** resource, and a time will come when it can no longer be relied on. Scientists are preparing for this time by exploring new technologies, such as fuel cells, which can reduce our reliance on oil. They are experimenting with ways to provide affordable **renewable** forms of energy, such as **biofuels**, solar energy, and wind energy.

In the United States, E85, a biofuel that is 85 percent ethanol, is a cheaper alternative to gasoline.

COMMODITY FACT!

China is consuming oil at a fast rate. Its demand for oil has doubled in the past decade as the country's major industries and transportation sectors grow. Half of this demand is met by importing oil from other parts of the world.

The Effect of Rising Prices

Some people believe that we may never truly run out of oil. They claim that as remaining oil supplies dwindle, the price of oil will rise accordingly. Eventually, oil will become so expensive that people will stop buying it, allowing what remains to continue to fuel the industries that need it the most, for many years to come. The rest of the population will turn to cheaper, more environmentally friendly alternatives.

Costly Environmental Considerations

It is often very costly for oil companies to meet government requirements that ensure their operations do not harm the environment. All aspects of oil exploration, extraction, and refining can be damaging. Exploring for oil and drilling can disrupt the seabed and affect the habitats of marine creatures. Oil spills can be devastating to natural ecosystems. The ability of oil companies to fund exploration and meet environmental standards will determine the extent to which new oil field discoveries will occur.

New Sources of Income

Some oil-producing countries with oil reserves running low have begun developing new sources of income. Middle Eastern countries, once heavily reliant on money generated from oil exports, are now developing other industries, such as tourism. Dubai, in the United Arab Emirates (UAE), has introduced luxury developments to bring in tourists and their money, including exclusive hotels, massive shopping centers, and even artificial resort islands.

Palm Islands is a luxury tourist resort that has been built off the coast of Dubai in the UAE. This photograph, taken from the *International Space Station*, shows its unique shape.

The Future of the Oil Industry

With the price of oil rising to record levels in recent years, consumers have started asking how much oil remains and how long it will last.

Peak Oil

In 1956, scientist M. King Hubbert developed the concept of peak oil, which proposed that there will come a time when the world reaches its maximum rate of oil extraction. After this time, the rate of oil extraction will gradually slow down.

Hubbert's Predictions

Hubbert made a number of predictions based on his peak oil theory. In 1956, he predicted that oil production in the United States would peak between 1965 and 1970, and he was right. Then, in 1974, Hubbert predicted that the global peak in oil production would be reached in 1995. Oil experts are still determining if Hubbert has been proved right or wrong.

New Predictions

Oil experts have different views on exactly when the world will reach peak oil. Some say it has happened already and that global oil production is declining. Others say we have not reached peak oil yet, but that it will occur within the next few years. One report, published by the UK Energy Research Center, states that the peak is likely to occur before 2030.

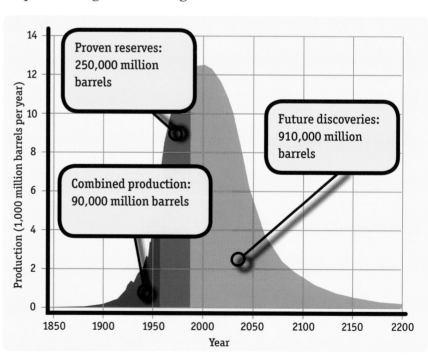

The concept of peak oil predicts that a time will come when global oil production reaches its maximum. It will then start declining.

The Effects of Reaching Peak Oil

When peak oil is reached, it will have a range of impacts.

- Countries that rely on oil-generated income will have to find new sources of income to support themselves.
- Transportation is likely to suffer in the short term as alternative fuels are developed to suit different engines and vehicles.
- Industries will then suffer as well if they are unable to transport their goods to destinations around the world.

Alternative Fuels

Alternative fuels, which currently exist, must be produced in amounts large enough to take the place of oil-based fuels. They must also be developed to suit different engines, vehicles, and industries. Developments in science suggest that this is possible, but that it will take time. Ultimately, the world will deal with the arrival of peak oil and will find ways to make up for the absence of oil, but the move from using fossil fuels to alternative fuels will be challenging.

In the future, biofuels may become an important substitute for gasoline to power the billions of cars on the road.

Find Out More

Web Sites for Further Information

- ### Oil basics
  Learn more about the formation of oil and the uses of oil.
  http://tonto.eia.doe.gov/kids/energy.cfm?page=oil_home

- ### Drilling for oil
  Learn more about how companies find and drill for oil.
  www.howstuffworks.com/oil-drilling.htm

- ### Refining oil
  Learn more about how oil is refined into fuel.
  www.howstuffworks.com/oil-refining.htm

- ### Alternatives to fossil fuels
  Learn more about possible alternatives to oil-based fuels.
  www.buzzle.com/articles/alternatives-to-fossil-fuels.html

Focus Questions

These questions might help you think about some of the issues raised in this book.

- What is likely to happen when major oil-producing regions reach peak oil?

- Which countries are likely to be most affected when supplies of oil are exhausted? Why?

- Is the role of OPEC beneficial to the global oil trade?

- Should drivers be offered incentives to run their cars on alternative fuels?

Glossary

agricultural	related to farming or used for farming
biofuels	fuels which are made from living things or their waste
demand	the amount of a product consumers want to buy
derricks	structures placed above oil wells to support the drill
developed countries	countries that are very industrialised
developing countries	countries in the early stages of becoming industrialised
domestic	relating to a person's own country
economy	a system that organises the production, distribution and exchange of goods and services, as well as incomes
ecosystems	communities of plants and animals that interact with one another and with the environments in which they live
export	a product which is sold to another country; or the action of sending a product to another country to sell it
fractions	parts that make up a chemical mixture
gas flares	tall pipes used to burn off waste gases
geologists	people who study the rocks and other substances that make up Earth's surface
greenhouse gases	gases found in the air that trap heat around Earth and cause higher temperatures
habitat	the natural environment of a plant or animal
imports	products which are bought or brought in from another country; or the action of buying and bringing a product into a country
natural resources	the naturally occurring useful wealth of a region or country, such as land, forests, coal, oil, gas and water
nonrenewable	from a source that will run out
organic compounds	chemicals that contain carbon
photosynthesis	the process by which plants use energy from the sun to convert carbon dioxide and water into sugar
renewable	from a source that will not run out
sediment	very tiny pieces of solid matter that settle at the bottom of a liquid
supply	the amount of a product that producers are able to sell
terrain	an area of land and its natural features

Index